LIVING TWO LIVES: DIFFERENTIATING YOUR PRIVATE AND CIVIC LIFE

Political Science for Grade 6 | Children's Reference Books

BABY PROFESSOR
EDUCATION KIDS

First Edition, 2020

Published in the United States by Speedy Publishing LLC, 40 E Main Street, Newark, Delaware 19711 USA.

© 2020 Baby Professor Books, an imprint of Speedy Publishing LLC

Baby Professor Books are available at special discounts when purchased in bulk for industrial and sales-promotional use. For details contact our Special Sales Team at Speedy Publishing LLC, 40 E Main Street, Newark, Delaware 19711 USA. Telephone (888) 248-4521 Fax: (210) 519-4043.

10 9 8 7 6 * 5 4 3 2 1

Print Edition: 9781541961036
Digital Edition: 9781541964037

See the world in pictures. Build your knowledge in style.
www.speedypublishing.com

Table Of Contents

We are not alone in the world. People belong to different places and groups. People have friends, acquaintances and relatives. People's lives can be broken down into two categories: private life and civic life. This book talks about the differences between the two categories.

People have friends, acquaintances and relatives.

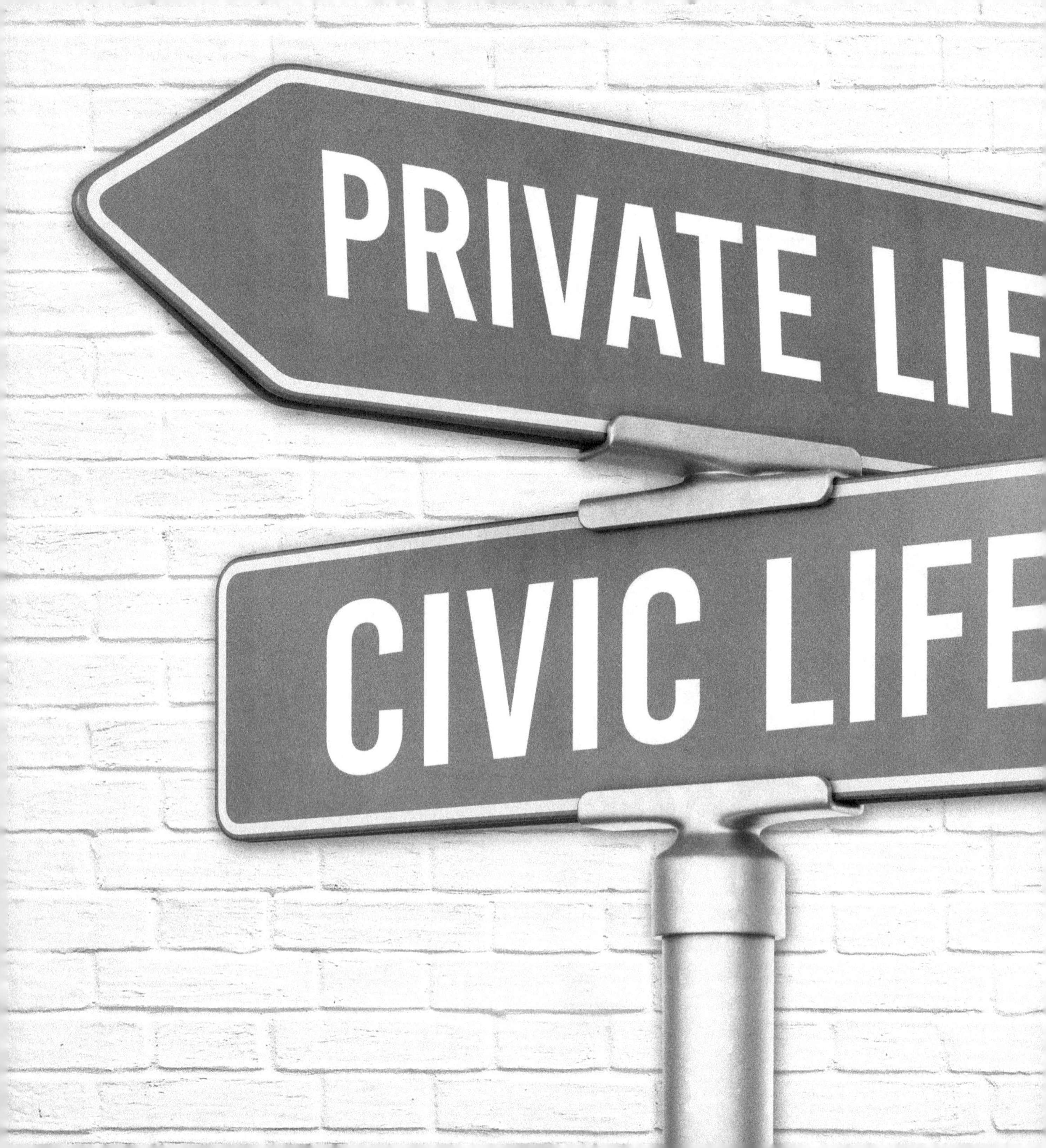
PRIVATE LIF
CIVIC LIFE

The Difference Between People's Private Lives and Their Civic Lives

People's private lives involve what they do alone or choose to do. It includes participating in activities that are chosen because of personal preference. It may be the hobby or hobbies that people have or it may include joining a club or association. For example, some people are interested in sports so they join a local sports team.

School kids playing football.

Learning how to play the guitar

Others are interested in music so they take private music lessons to learn how to play a musical instrument.

The time that people spend socializing with family or friends is done in people's private lives. This may include family get togethers or attending a friend's birthday party, for example.

Family having a garden party in the summer.

a woman sitting uder a tree in a park, reading a book.

Even the time that a person chooses to spend alone is done as a choice made in a person's private life.

The beliefs, customs, religious affiliation and opinions are all considered to be the choices that people make in their private lives. Whatever people do in their free time all falls under the category of private life.

A young man praying to God at home.

A group of volunteers with garbage bags cleaning an area in a park.

People's civic lives, on the other hand, extend further. It involves engaging in civic matters. This engagement occurs when people take part in duties in their neighborhood, town, city or country. Any contributions that people make to issues that affect the conditions or quality of life for themselves are examples of what happens in civic life.

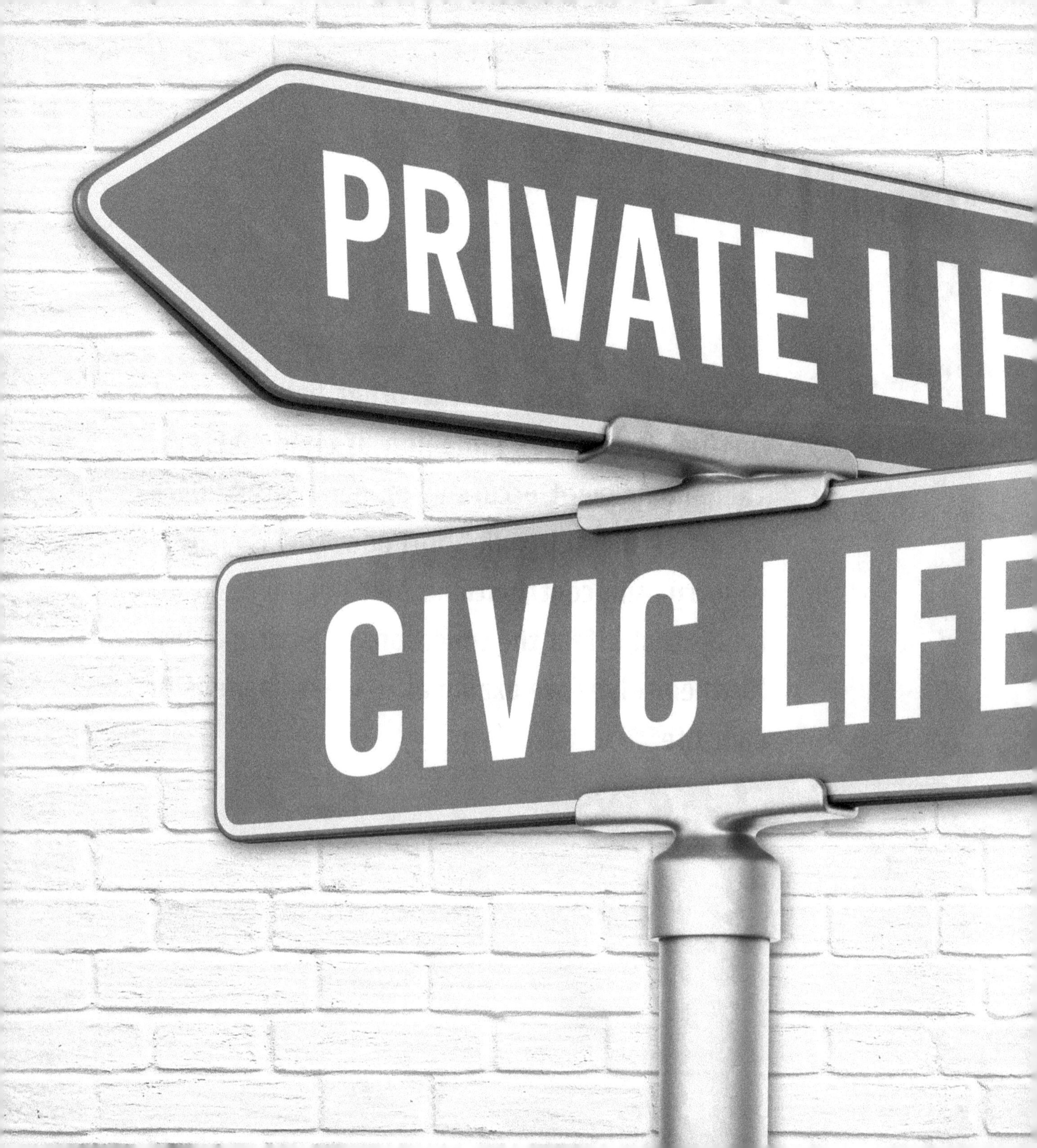
PRIVATE LIF
CIVIC LIFE

Ways in Which People Engage in Civic Life

There are many different types of civic engagement. When people are still in childhood, their civic engagement is naturally restricted by age. However, there are still things that a minor can do. Children can take notice of what is happening around their neighborhood. There are organizations in which volunteer work can be done. Volunteering is an excellent way to make a positive contribution to other people's lives.

Young volunteers and children
collecting garbage on the beach.

Volunteers with children sorting donation goods

Becoming aware of the current events in one's own neighborhood or state is also a good way to start to discover aspects of civic life. Every municipality has concerns and issues. By learning about what is happening in society, people can come together to find solutions.

Areas such as community safety and environmental protection, for example, are just two ways of how a young person can engage in civic life. By getting involved and working together, people's talents are pooled and the entire community can benefit. Being aware of the political and social organizations in one's local area is a good way for a young person's civic participation to start.

Kids with volunteers planting trees in a park.

Diverse crowd of people

Showing respect and treating other members of society courteously can go a long way in maintaining civility. The United States is a large country that is made up of people from different ethnic backgrounds. Understanding that all citizens are equal and have the same rights is very important.

People of any age have the right to know the structure of their government. Young people can learn about political parties for youth and membership into the party. All of this is a part of people's civic participation.

Young people can learn about political parties for youth and membership into the party.

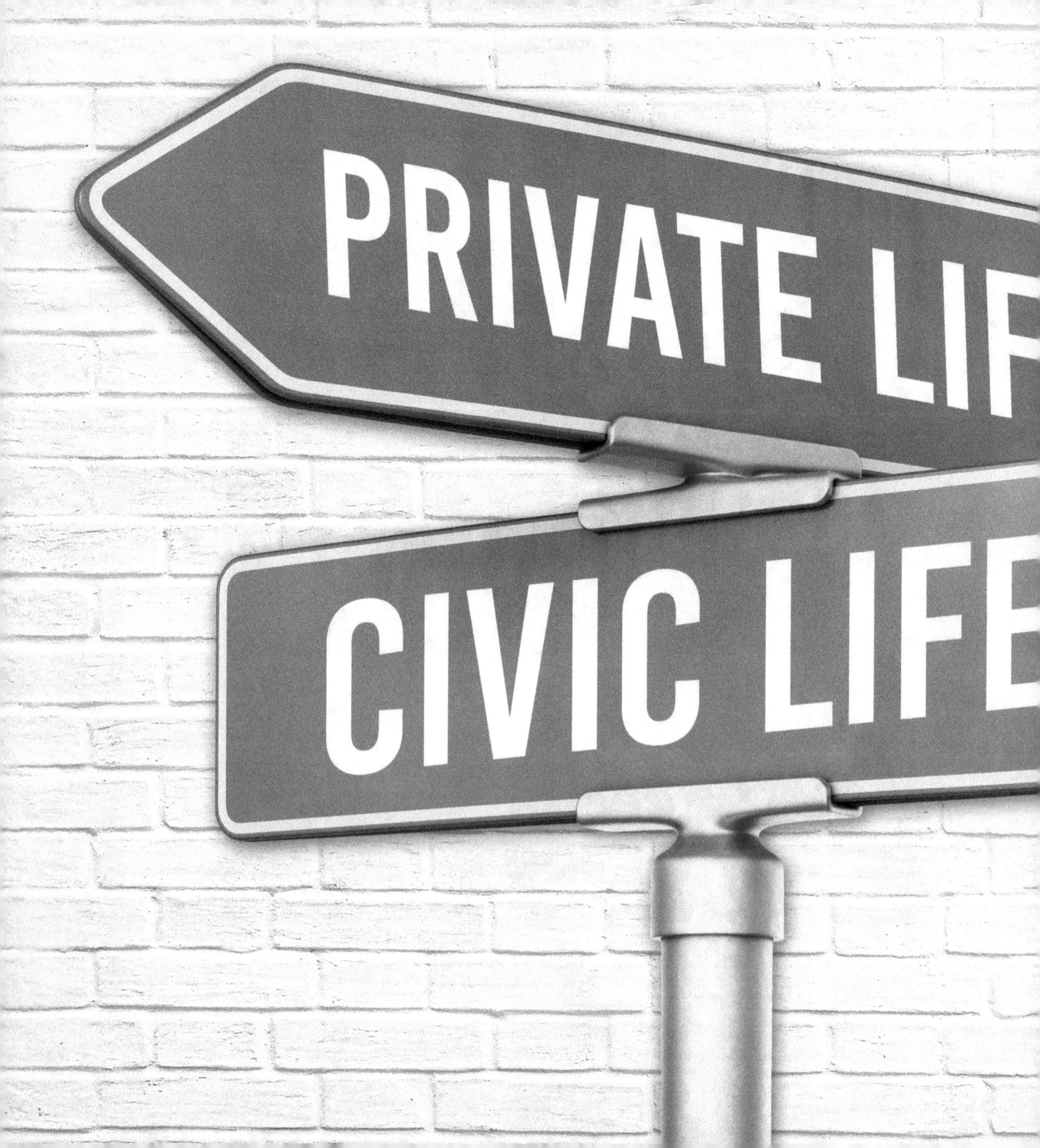
PRIVATE LIF
CIVIC LIF

Levels of Government in the United States of America and how Understanding Them can Influence Civic Participation

In the United States, the federal government has power over the entire country. Governments at the state level control what happens in an individual state while local governments govern local municipalities such as cities or towns.

In the US, the federal government has power over the entire country.

The symbols of US politcal parties: the democrat donkey and republican elephant

There are two main political parties in the United States. They are the Democratic Party and the Republican Party.

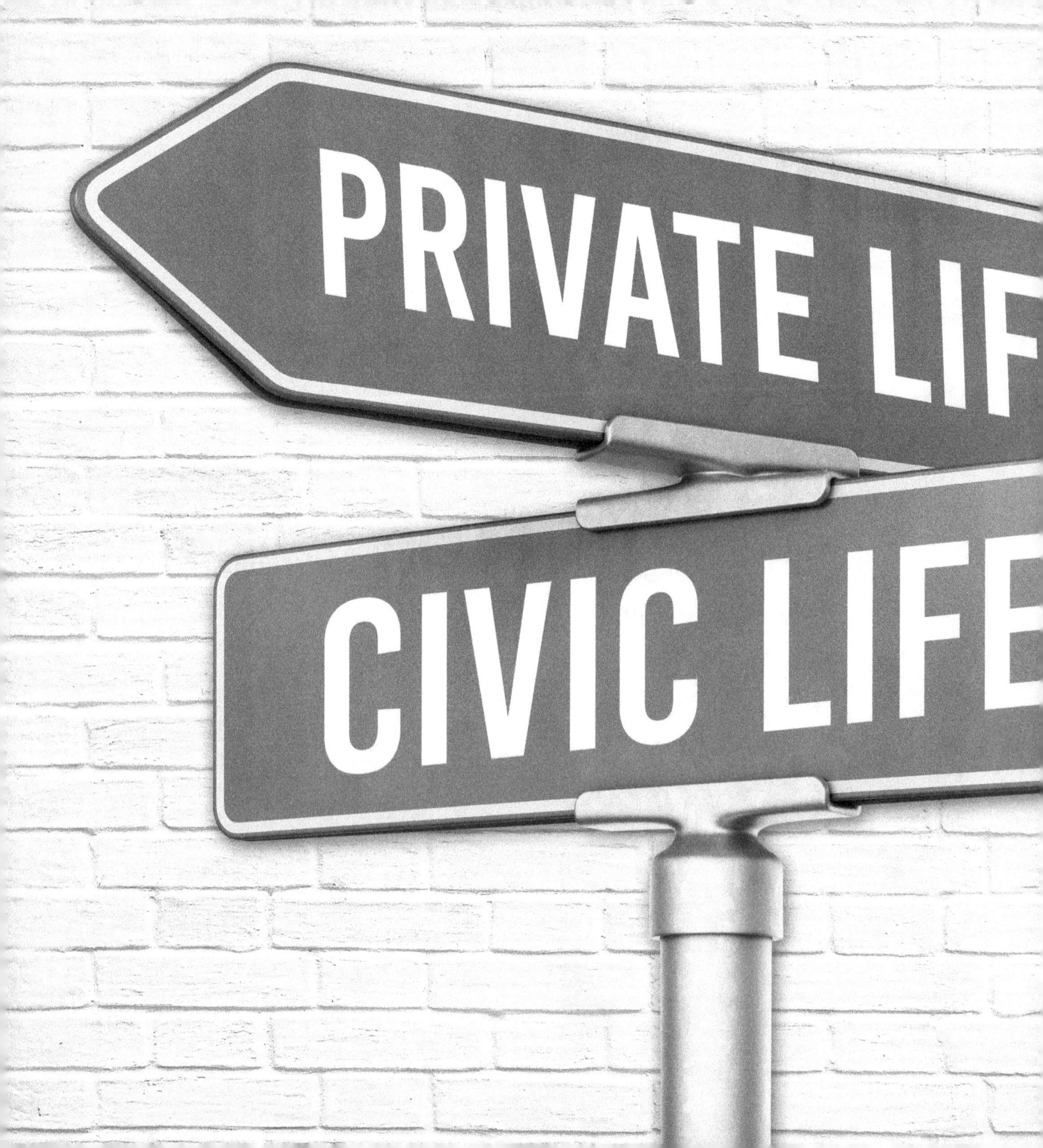
PRIVATE LIF
CIVIC LIFE

The Structure of the Government of the United States

The federal government of the United Sates, as per the Constitution, is divided into three branches. This breakdown is done so that power can be shared by all three branches. The three branches of government are: The Legislative, The Executive and the Judicial. Each branch has its own obligations.

3 BRANCHES *of* U.S. GOVERNMENT

★ ★ ★ ★

 Constitution
(provided a separation of powers)

Legislative
(makes laws)

Executive
(carries out laws)

Judicial
(interprets laws)

 Congress

 Senate

 House of Representatives

 President

 Vice President

 Cabinet

 Supreme Court

 Other Federal Courts

The U.S. Capitol Building in Washington DC is the home of the US Congress, and the seat of the legislative branch of the U.S. federal government.

The Legislative, which contains Congress, the House of Representatives and the Senate, is responsible for making laws.

The Executive, which consists of the president, vice president, the Cabinet and other national agencies, is responsible for implementing the laws.

The President and the First Family live
in the White House in Washington, D.C.

The Judicial, which includes the courts, has the duty of evaluating the laws. The highest and most powerful court is called the Supreme Court. A Supreme Court is presided over by a justice, who the president of the United States appoints. Other courts have judges who preside over them. These judges are not appointed but instead are voted in by citizens who reside in their local areas.

Although each branch has its own duties, either of the other two branches can exercise the right to make amendment to decisions made by the other branches.

GOVERNMENT

LEGISLATIVE

makes laws

EXECUTIVE

carries out laws

JUDICIAL

evaluates laws

An overview of the functions of three branches of the US government.

Flags of the US states.

In addition to the federal government, there are state governments. State governments are broken down into the same three branches into which the federal government is divided. They have their own administration and carry out their own laws. However, the Constitution and federal law supersede state laws. The head of a state is the governor.

The level of government in the United States which falls under the state level is a local government. It is common for a local government to consist of two areas. They include municipalities and counties, with counties being further broken down into townships.

City Hall with American flag in Texas.

United States Declaration of Independence, Constitution and Bill of Rights

Being knowledgeable of the history of one's country, state or city can help shape how a person responds to civic life. People are influenced by their history and society. There are three very important documents that have greatly led to the freedom and rights of all Americans. They are the Declaration of Independence, the Constitution of the United States of America and the Bill of Rights.

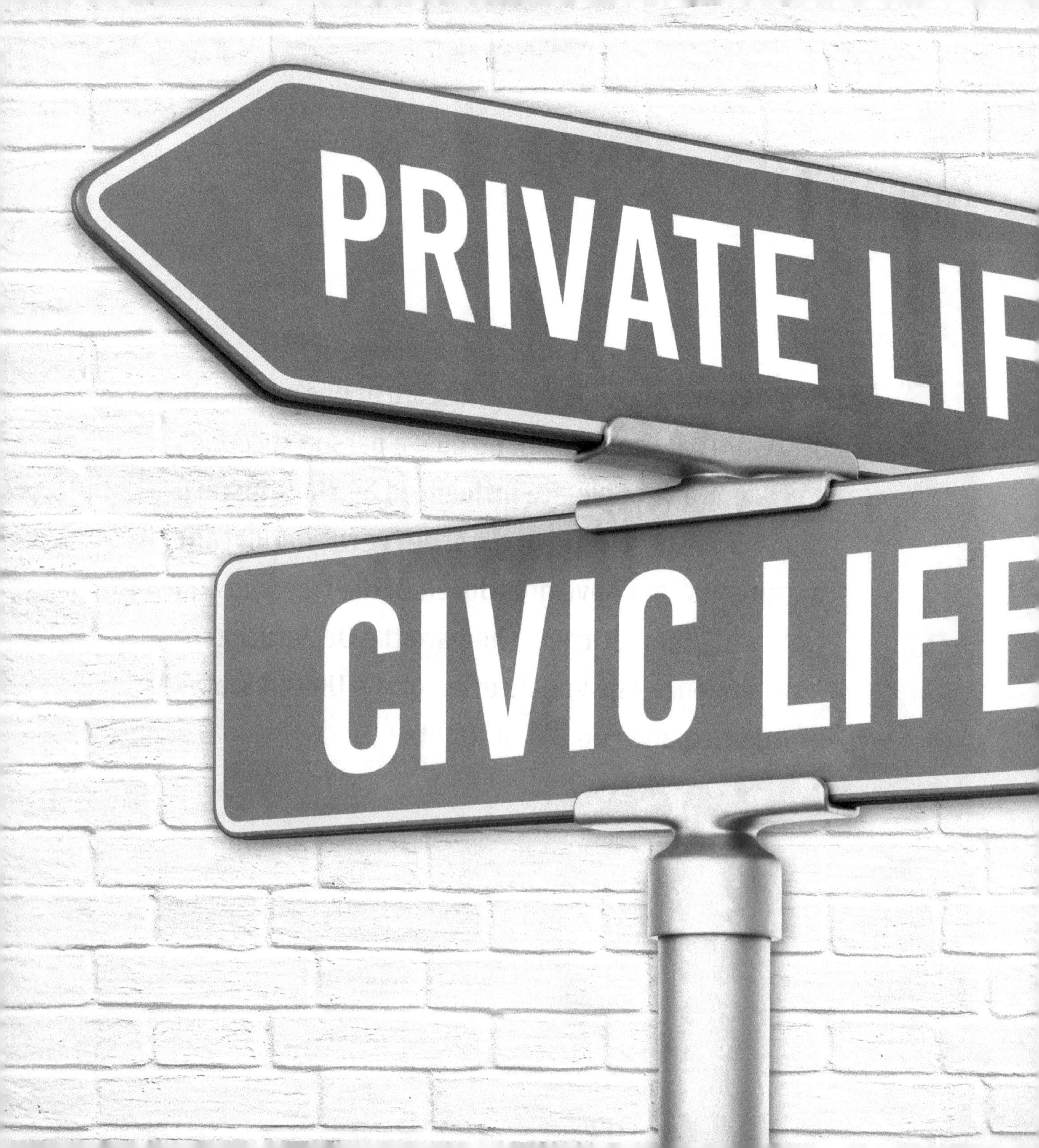
PRIVATE LIF
CIVIC LIFE

The Declaration of Independence, the Constitution of the United States of America and the Bill of Rights

The Declaration of Independence was established on July 4, 1776. This declaration states that all citizens are equal and it is the people themselves who empower the government. It holds to the principle that the people's rights cannot be ignored or taken away by the government.

The signing of the United States
Declaration of Independence in 1776.

"We the People" are the opening words of the preamble to the Constitution of the USA.

The constitution of the United States was granted formal consent in June, 1788. It allowed for the people of the United States to be governed by a democratic government. Liberty and equality were to be given to all citizens. The constitution allowed for power to be in the hands of government at both the federal and state levels. By dividing power, individual states could focus their attention to their own concerns and their governance could thereby be tailored to meet the needs of their constituents. The federal government would then be enabled to govern the country as a whole.

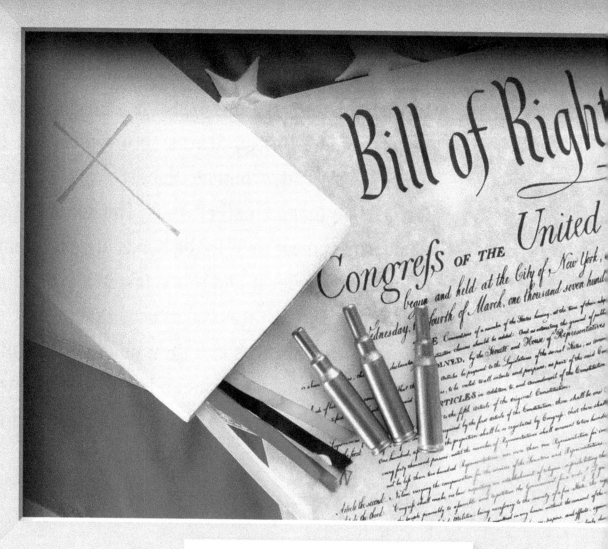

United States Bill of Rights

The Bill of Rights came into existence in 1791. The idea for the drafting of the bill was by the American people. They wanted to have a document that details their freedoms and rights. They wanted to make sure that there was no room for ambiguity that may result in their rights and freedoms not being officially guaranteed. The Bill of Rights is the official guarantee that the government cannot take away the rights of an individual American citizen. In the beginning, it started out with ten amendments.

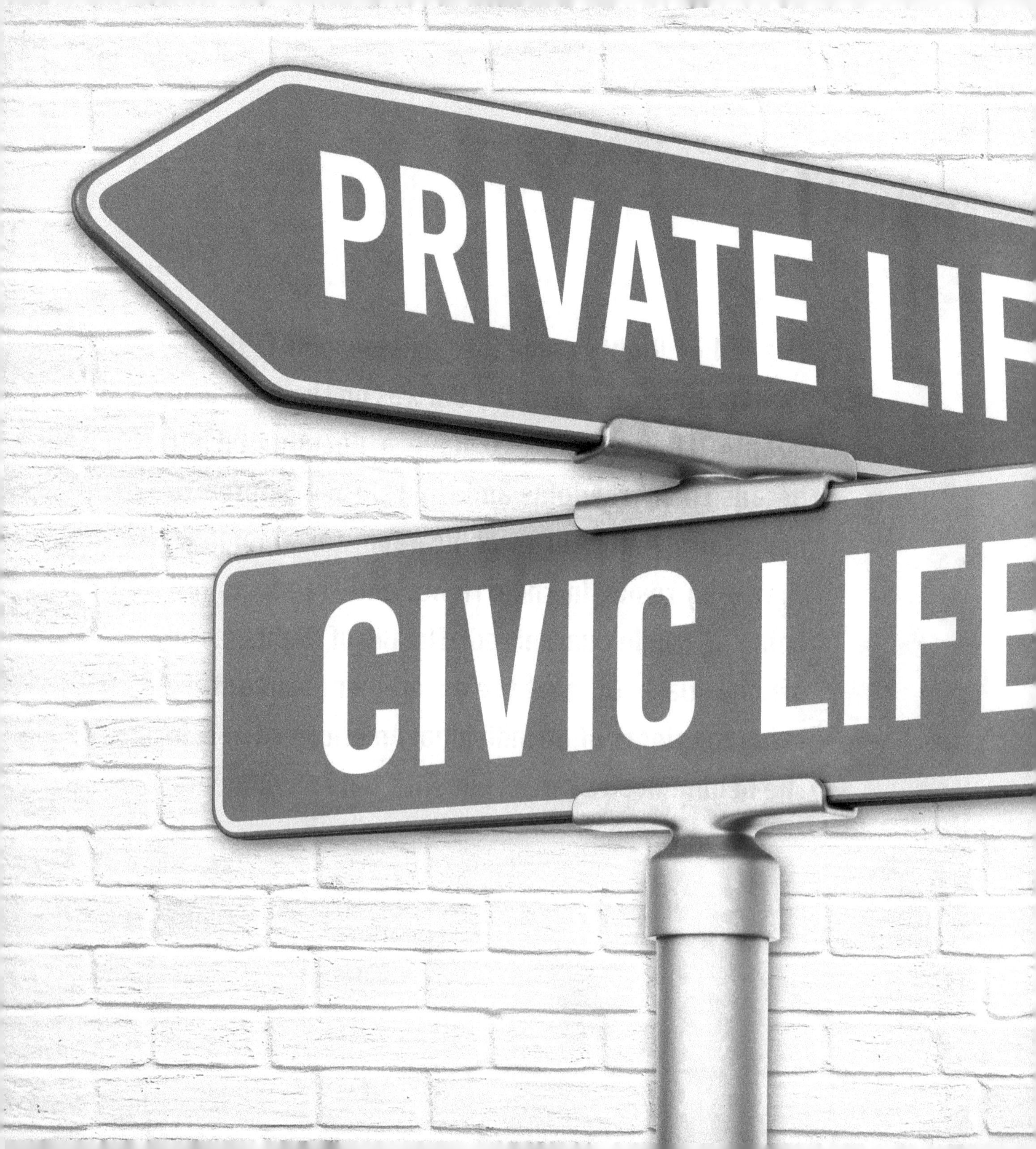
PRIVATE LIF
CIVIC LIF

The Right to Vote

American citizens have the right to vote for candidates who are running for office. The right to vote comes at the age of eighteen years. One way that people can engage in a civic matter is to exercise their right to vote. Before casting a vote, it is important for people to make informed decisions. Voters can educate themselves on the platform or reasons why a candidate should be elected into office. It is the voters, or the ordinary citizens, who play vital roles during elections. American citizens are free to decide on how they wish to engage in civic life. Every vote counts!

One way that people can engage in a civic matter is to exercise their right to vote.

Two young adult women exercising their right to vote.

One very important vote is who becomes the president of the United States. There is a specific process involved in electing the president. It is a very long process that involves the participation of many people. Thus, there are many opportunities for people to engage in civic duties. Like the election of the president, in a democratic society, citizens have the right to vote for candidates in other levels of government. Taking part in the various stages of the election process or voting in an election are important ways in which civic participation can occur.

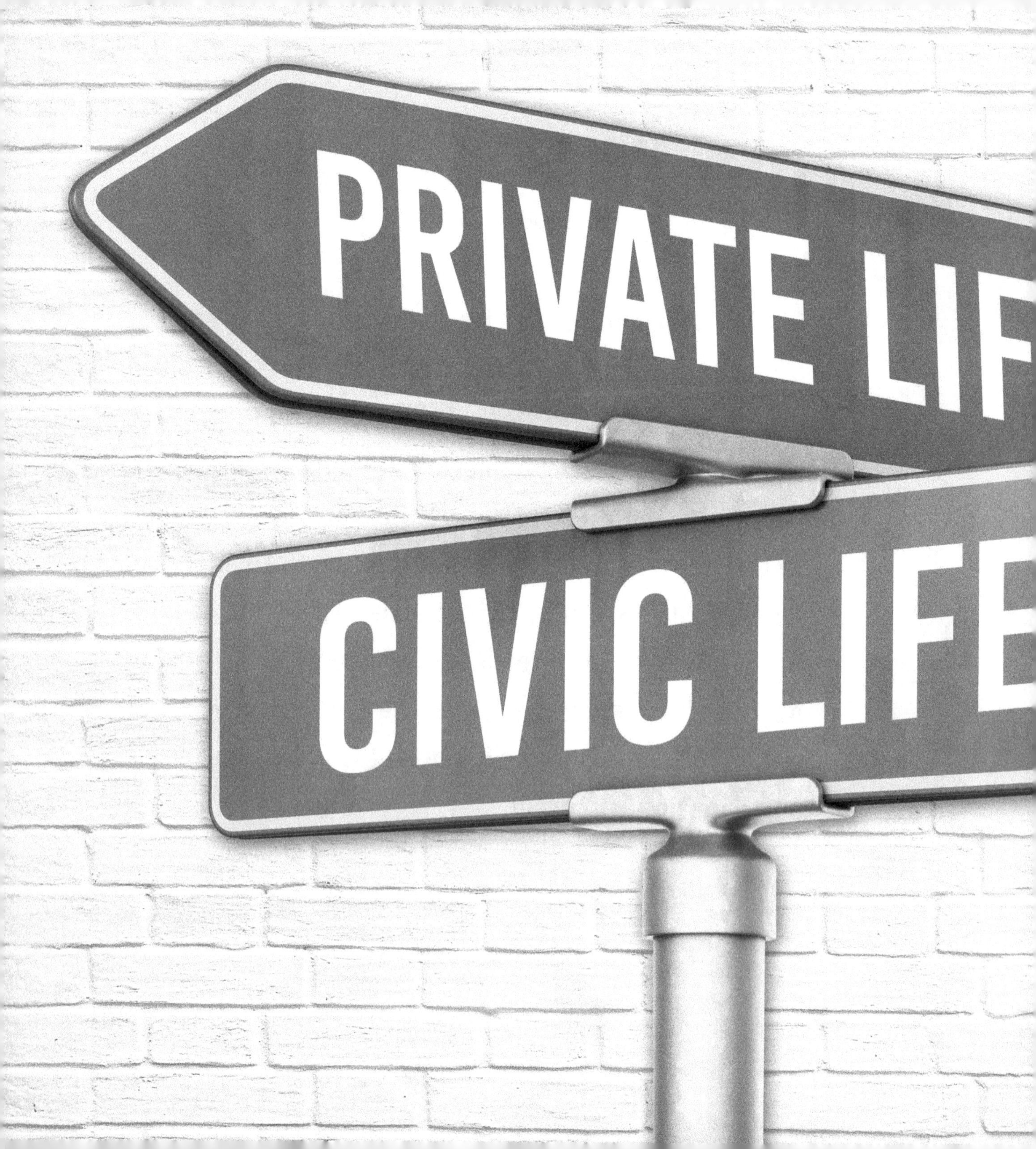
PRIVATE LIF
CIVIC LIF

The Election Process for the Presidency

There are many stages to the election process for the presidency of the United States of America. A brief description of each stage is as follows:

To run in an election means that a person has decided to become a candidate. Many months prior to the actual elections, the Democratic Party and the Republican Party start what is known as *campaign trails*. Each party has a group of people who form a team. The members of the team tour the country to try to gain support from people and to raise funds for their campaigns.

Members of the campaign team tour the country to gain support and raise funds for campaigns.

One very important part of the campaign is
for the candidates to participate in a debate.

One very important part of the campaign is for the candidates to participate in a debate. During the debate, each candidate is expected to supply answers to very important questions so that the public can know what each candidate thinks of certain issues. Each candidate is also expected to demonstrate their view on current issues and policies.

Following the debate, which is shown on different media, there is a primary election. In this gathering, members of the party say the name of the candidate for whom they would like to vote. Alternatively, some states have a caucus. The difference with a caucus is that the gathering is closed when members of the political party choose the candidate.

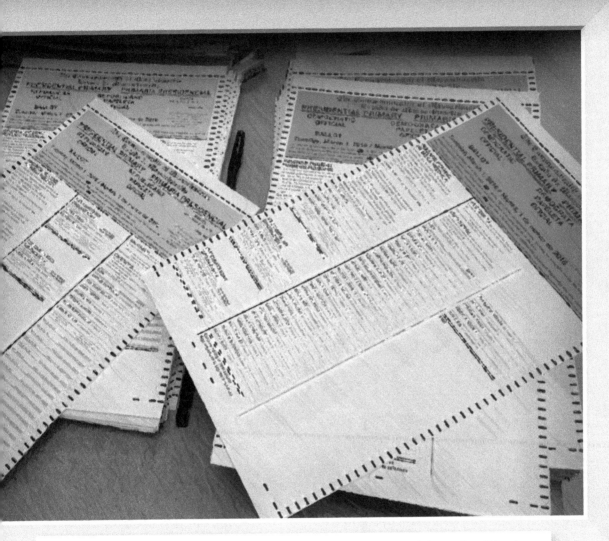

A photo of presidential primary election ballots

Confetti and streamers are released
at a Democratic National Convention

Following the primaries and caucuses, a national convention is held. At this convention, each party will nominate one person to be their presidential nominee. A few months later the presidential nominee will choose a person who s/he would like to fill the role of vice president. This person is called the *running mate.* If the presidential nominee wins the election, the running mate becomes the vice president. Following this, national conventions are held and the presidential nominees are announced.

Once this takes place, there is a process called the *Electoral College*. During the Electoral College, each state gets to cast their vote. Votes are cast in proportion to the population of the state. To win, a minimum of 270 electoral votes is needed out of the 538 electors.

UNITED STATES
ELECTORAL COLLEGE

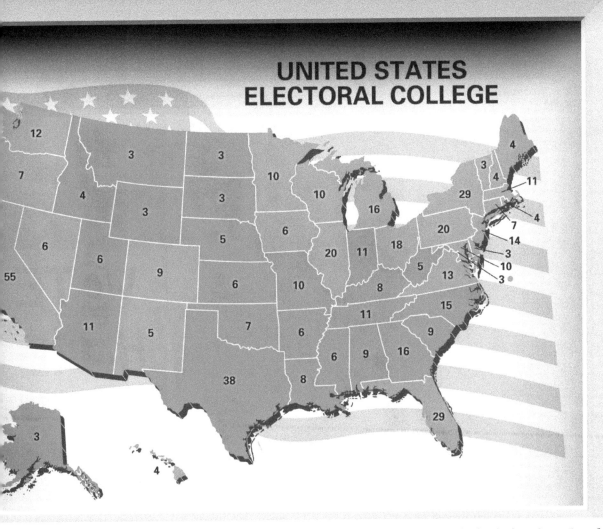

lectoral votes allocated to each state and to the District of Columbia.
The colors red and blue represent different political parties.

Group Of Young People Standing At
The Entrance Of a Voting place.

Finally, the General Election is held. Each American citizen will have the chance to cast a vote. It is important that all people turn up to vote because, except for in Nebraska and Maine, the electoral votes will automatically go to the candidate who receives the majority of the people's votes. The president of the United States is determined by the presidential nominee who receives the most electoral votes.

People have a private life and a civic life. Although the two can be separately named, the values from one quite often influence the decisions made in the other. To be a good citizen, people need to know their history, their form of government and what they can do to make a difference in their town, their state, their country and even the world.

Visit

www.speedypublishing.com

To view and download free content
on your favorite subject and browse
our catalog of new and exciting
books for readers of all ages.

CPSIA information can be obtained
at www.ICGtesting.com
Printed in the USA
BVHW062048280121
599006BV00005B/436